Contents

THE STORY OF
Medicine
by EDMUND HUNTER
with illustrations by ROBERT AYTON

Publishers: Ladybird Books Ltd . Loughborough
© Ladybird Books Ltd (formerly Wills & Hepworth Ltd) 1972
Printed in England

Before history began

It has long been known that Man descended from ape-like ancestors. The process of evolution spanned many hundreds of thousands of years. Gradually he came down from the trees, learned to walk on two feet, lost much of his physical strength and, instead, developed a bigger head and brain.

The earliest humans lived on the cold, wet ground which they shared with the many strange and dangerous animals that inhabited the Earth at that time. They hunted for their food, using as weapons the teeth and horns of the beasts they killed and the skins to cover their naked bodies. They lived in small family groups, had no recognised form of speech but communicated with each other by grunts, gestures and punches.

As the years went by our prehistoric ancestors made three important discoveries. They found that a sharpened piece of flint could be turned into a useful tool or weapon, and later they were able to fit a handle to it, making it easier to wield. The discovery of fire was a further advance. Man could then warm and dry himself as well as cook his food. Fire was a means of protection too, because it helped to keep wild animals away.

4   **Early man shelters from the cold**

0 7214 0333 6

Medicine by instinct

Early man, like the apes before him and the animals all around, was subject to illness, injury and death. Life was uncomfortable, dangerous and hard, and the average span of life was probably little more than thirty years. If he developed a sore or wound his instinctive action was to suck or lick the affected place. He found that bleeding sometimes eased the pain of a wound. Stomach ache, after too big a feast, could be helped by massaging with the hands.

Implements normally employed as weapons could be used to cut off mutilated limbs. It was noticed that fire, when used to cauterise wounds, seemed to prevent them from becoming fatal – if the patient survived the shock!

The small family groups broadened into larger communities. Germs and viruses had more opportunity to spread and breed in human bodies. Disease increased, as it does today in closely-living, unhygienic communities.

Instinctive medical activities later developed into ceremonial rituals which became as important as healing itself. They were performed by the leader of the community or tribe whenever a person became ill.

Cauterising a wound

The medicine-man

Medicine progressed slowly and very painfully along two lines, the magical and the practical. Sometimes the two were linked together, sometimes they were carried on separately. The medicine-man came into being to cure the mental and physical ills of the people, or to kill off a patient thought to be incurable and a burden to the rest of the community.

Magic was practised to drive out the evil spirits which were thought to cause disease. It took many forms, including the use of objects coated with special substances or carved with mystical designs to give them supposedly magical powers. Gifts and sacrifices might be offered to the appropriate spirit. Some rituals involved the amputation of a finger or other organ.

Excavations of Stone Age settlements have uncovered skulls into which a circular hole had been cut. This operation is known as trepanning and was probably carried out because it was thought that an evil spirit could escape, so relieving the patient of some mental disorder. Signs that the bone around the hole had, in some cases, begun to heal suggest that the sufferer had managed to survive the surgery. The circular pieces of bone removed from the skulls of unfortunate mental patients were possibly made into necklaces and worn as charms, or amulets, to ward off other evil spirits.

An operation in Stone Age times

Early developments

As the centuries passed, man gained an elementary knowledge of anatomy from the animals he killed. He travelled great distances on foot and learned about nature. He found a method of counting, using his fingers and toes, invented the wheel and discovered how to grow plants and make pottery. He found that he could cure minor ailments by taking herbs, applying mud plasters, massaging and dieting. More troublesome diseases were treated by magic, bleeding or amputation. The medicine-man was the central figure of the tribe and as it gradually grew larger and larger his importance grew with it.

Between 7000 and 4000 B.C., whole civilisations developed from the early tribes. Diseases multiplied in number and variety but only little progress was made in treating them.

Around 3000 B.C. knowledge gradually increased in the civilisations that were developing in Egypt and Mesopotamia, around the fertile valleys of the rivers Nile and Euphrates. Medicine became the job of specialist physicians who were paid for their work, but who were severely punished, sometimes by death, if the patient received an injury or died.

Medical treatments included fumigation (smoking out the patient through the back passage, mouth and nose), many herbal remedies and the application of animal urine, excreta and powdered bones!

In the treatment of minor ailments, herbs were used for many centuries

Ancient Egypt

The Ancient Egyptians, who were among the earliest civilised people in the world, were also among the first to make a serious study of the human body. Their custom of embalming and preserving the bodies of important people before they were buried provided a natural opportunity for their studies. It was the practice, during the embalming process, to remove the main internal organs such as the stomach, liver, kidneys, heart and lungs, and place them in separate jars. In this way the position of these parts within the body was learned.

Although magic still played an important part in curing, or attempting to cure, certain kinds of illness, practical methods were also developed by the Egyptians. The physicians found that wounds would heal better if the edges of the flesh were held together. Splints and bandages were used for broken limbs, and dislocated joints were reset. Generally speaking, magic was cheap and used on the ordinary people while the more expensive practical methods were reserved for royalty and other high-born individuals.

Many effective medicines were used in Egypt but it was still thought that 'evil spirits' were discouraged by such substances as bull's blood, snake fat and human excreta.

The Egyptians could write, and the availability of a material known as papyrus enabled them to record their discoveries and treatments for future generations.

bove - A wealthy dignitary of
~araoh's court has intelligent
~atment for a broken leg, instead
~ the witch doctor magic that
~uld have been used on a
~ember of the lower classes.

~ght - Ancient model
~ a sheep's liver used
~ Babylonian doctors
~ predict the course
~ an illness.

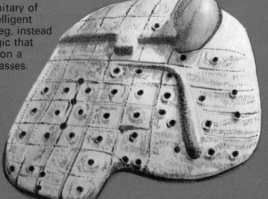

Other early civilisations

Although the civilisations of Mesopotamia and, more especially, Egypt were possibly the most important, others were also flourishing around the same period. They each added their contribution to the general store of medical knowledge.

In India, around the valley of the River Indus, physicians discovered the importance of the pulse. Over one thousand diseases were diagnosed and more than one hundred surgical instruments were available for operations. Patients undergoing surgery were even hypnotised to ease the pain.

The Hebrews practised hygiene to prevent disease and were therefore the first people to introduce a system of public health. Animals killed for food were first bled so that disease thought to be carried in the blood would not be passed on to the consumer.

Medicine in China began about 2800 B.C. Its most important contribution to our modern civilisation was the process of *acupuncture*. By puncturing appropriate areas of the body with special, very fine needles, the Chinese believed that the body could be helped back to health. Although acupuncture is not generally recognised by the medical profession, it is still practised by specially-trained people all over the world today and achieves cures which cannot be explained by usual medical science. The Chinese also discovered nearly two thousand medicinal substances.

A traditional Chinese acupuncture diagram and ancient model, showing some of the hundreds of needle points still used in acupuncture

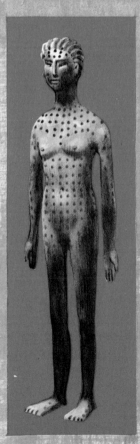

Greece

During the period around 600 B.C. the medical knowledge built up in Egypt gradually spread to Greece where, for the next few hundred years it was further developed.

Greek warriors knew how to remove an enemy's arrows from their bodies, stop the bleeding and apply healing substances. If a warrior was lucky and did not develop some form of infection in the wound he would recover to fight another day. Infection was a subject about which nothing was known and many of the wounded died from this cause.

The most useful contributions to Greek medicine were made by the great philosophers. Names like Pythagoras – what schoolboy or girl has not heard of him – Hippocrates, Socrates, Plato and Aristotle were all connected with the advance of science and medicine. Much of the work they carried out was not improved upon until as late as the 15th century. Some medical treatment was also carried on by priests in the temples but this was generally of the magical rather than the practical kind.

Most important of all the Greek achievements was the ability to diagnose illnesses by observation and deduction, to use powers of reasoning to explain the cause of a disease instead of relying on old superstitious ideas about evil spirits.

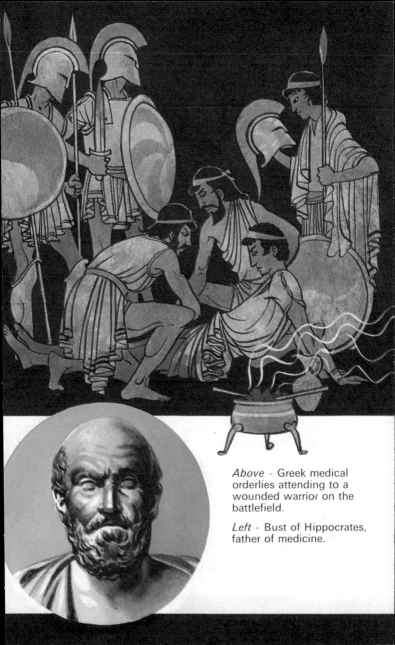

Above - Greek medical orderlies attending to a wounded warrior on the battlefield.

Left - Bust of Hippocrates, father of medicine.

The Father of Medicine

Of all the Greek doctors, Hippocrates was the most notable. He is often called the Father of Medicine and some of his ideas are still important. Many students who qualify as doctors today take what is known as the Hippocratic Oath; a collection of promises, drawn up by Hippocrates, which forms the basis of our medical code of honour.

Hippocrates of Cos was born about 460 B.C. on the island of Cos off the coast of Asia Minor. He established medical schools in Athens and elsewhere and wrote several books as well as many medical case histories. He believed that disease was a natural process produced by natural causes and should be treated by exercise, massage, salt water baths, diet and suitable medicines. He observed diseases such as pneumonia, pleurisy, tuberculosis and malaria, and added to the medical language words like chronic, relapse, crisis and convalescence.

One of Hippocrates' theories was that the body consisted of four 'humours' or fluids; blood, phlegm, yellow bile and black bile. Too much of one fluid, he believed, would cause disease and it was the doctors' job to restore the balance. It was not until some two-thousand years later that the theory was proved incorrect.

Hippocrates reads the Oath to some of his students

Roman times

Around 300 B.C. the Roman legions conquered the Mediterranean area, Greece, Asia Minor, Syria, Judea and Egypt. At first the practice of medicine was left to slaves and Greek doctors, but later the Romans became very efficient in the practice of medicine and surgery. Some surgical instruments found in the ruins of Pompeii were so efficiently designed as to closely resemble modern ones.

Perhaps the most important advances made by the Romans were in their public health systems. Inspectors supervised the sale of food in the markets and the first hospitals were opened. Great aqueducts brought water into the city of Rome and fine public baths were built so that people could keep themselves clean. There were flush lavatories, sewers, fountains and wells. However, very poor people still had to bathe in the River Tiber, and outside the cities, towns and villages were filthy with rubbish. Nevertheless, the Romans were the best-washed people in the whole ancient world.

Enclosed
Watercourse

Road

2000 years ago fourteen of these great
aqueducts brought 300,000,000 gallons of
water into Rome each day, supplying the
city's public, water-flushed lavatories, and
great public baths, each of which could take
up to 2000 bathers at a time. Public health in
Rome was of a very high standard, owing
everything to this continued supply of cool
and clean water.

*Black diagram shows cross section
of aqueduct.*

The Dark Ages

The Romans had nearly two hundred surgical instruments; they performed plastic surgery and developed a form of anaesthetic to give some relief to patients undergoing operations. This consisted of a sponge soaked in special juices, placed in the patient's mouth. The liquid dripped down the throat and caused drowsiness. Dentists provided their patients with sets of teeth wired together. These were real teeth, not false ones.

With the defeat of the Roman Empire by the barbarians in the 5th century, civilisation became centered in the eastern half of Europe, where the old Greek ideas still survived. The capital of the area was Byzantium, later to be known as Constantinople and now Istanbul. Medical progress here was desperately slow. The Muslims, who chiefly populated the area, relied on information contained in the books of Hippocrates which were translated into Arabic.

In England, after the departure of the Romans about 400 A.D., the invading Anglo-Saxons neglected the Roman baths and public health systems, and medical treatment declined.

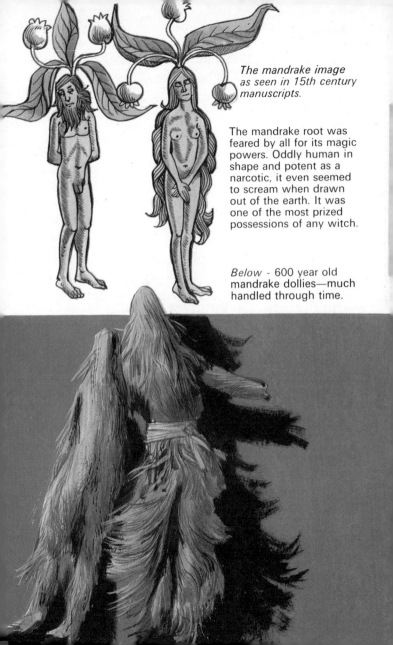

The mandrake image as seen in 15th century manuscripts.

The mandrake root was feared by all for its magic powers. Oddly human in shape and potent as a narcotic, it even seemed to scream when drawn out of the earth. It was one of the most prized possessions of any witch.

Below - 600 year old mandrake dollies—much handled through time.

Plagues

During the later Middle Ages, a period of history which roughly spanned the four hundred years between 1000 and 1400 A.D., disease was generally considered to be a punishment for sin or was something that just had to be endured. Monasteries were the centres of learning but few monks studied medicine. Ignorance again prevailed and the teachings of Hippocrates were almost forgotten.

The dreaded disease of leprosy, which had been widespread for hundreds of years, was controlled not by medical means but by confining poor lepers to colonies and rich ones to their estates, away from other people. This was the one important advance in public health during the period.

During this period, plagues ravaged Europe, killing nearly half the population, and the Black Death struck Britain in 1348. Nobody knew how to deal with it. The advice of doctors was to run away from the affected areas. If that was not possible they suggested rest and quiet, purging the body, purifying the air with fire, soothing the humours or letting blood. Everybody agreed, however, that the plague was Heaven's punishment for the sinfulness of man.

The Black Death ended a dark period of medical history in which little real progress had been made for twelve hundred years.

Carrying away the dead during the Black Death

A.D. 1400 — 1500

As the Middle Ages drew to an end, public health was being taken more seriously. Officials inspected food as well as the herbal remedies prepared by the apothecaries (chemists), and supervised the cleaning of some streets. Hospitals and universities were built in large numbers. About 1450 Johann Gutenberg invented printing by movable type, and books could then be produced more cheaply and in greater quantities. Medical knowledge from different countries could be properly recorded, studied and compared.

At that time doctors were very often highly-educated men, well-respected in the community. Surgeons were considered to be of much lower breed. They did their work in public places or among the wounded on the battlefield, where the newly-invented guns and cannon were causing dreadful injuries. They were joined by barbers, butchers and even executioners in the process of letting blood and the removal of teeth. Some 'quacks' specialised in conjuring tricks by which they pretended to remove bloodstained pebbles from the heads of mental patients!

Although the practice of medicine improved further between the 15th and 16th centuries, surgery was still a barbarous and painful practice in which patients often suffered more from the treatment than they did from their original complaints.

A 16th century physician and assistants prepare to amputate the limb of a terrified patient in the presence of his family

Studying the human body

Even as far back as Roman times people had a fear of dead bodies. Dissection, that is the cutting open of bodies to learn more about the various parts and how they work, was banned by the religious authorities and by law. This delayed the study of anatomy for over a thousand years.

It is perhaps strange that the first real effort to study the human body was made by Renaissance artists such as Michelangelo, Raphael and, in particular, Leonardo da Vinci. Leonardo wished to draw the body with more realism than had previously been done and so he carefully examined the shape of the bone structure and muscles. Not satisfied with this he dissected over thirty dead bodies himself and drew pictures of most of the internal organs as well as the veins and arteries.

Later, a doctor named Andreas Vesalius turned the study of anatomy into a proper and recognised practice. In order to obtain subjects for his early examinations he had to steal the corpses of criminals and highwaymen which were left hanging on roadside gallows after public executions. A native of Brussels, Vesalius trained as a doctor in Paris, later moving to Padua University, northern Italy, where he became Professor of Anatomy. In 1543 he had published an illustrated book – The Working of the Human Body.

Removing the dead bodies of executed criminals
for dissection

Blood and air

The next important advance in medical knowledge came in 1627 when an English doctor, William Harvey, discovered how blood flowed through the body. As a member of St. Bartholomew's hospital, in London, he carried out numerous experiments on animals and human bodies and finally arrived at the correct conclusion that the heart is a pump which forces blood outward through the arteries to all parts of the body, the veins then carrying the circulating blood back to the heart again. He also found that valves in the heart allowed the blood to flow only in one direction.

Later in the same century another great discovery was made. This time it was a chemist, not a doctor, who made it. He was an Englishman named Robert Boyle, who found that air had substance and could be measured and weighed. In the following century an Englishman, Joseph Priestley and a Frenchman, Antoine Lavoisier, working separately, found that air was a mixture of oxygen and nitrogen and that the harder the body worked the more air it needed to keep it going.

However, despite these discoveries, the 17th century ended and the 18th century began without any great changes in the treatment of illness. Bleeding, purging and dieting were still the popular remedies. Smallpox became the most dreaded disease.

Above - For many centuries blood-letting was regarded as a positive cure for many ills, sometimes—alas—with tragic results. The illustration shows a 15th century physician with two patients.

Right - William Harvey, 1578-1657, discoverer of the circulation of the blood.

Physical and mental health

A great change came over Britain, Europe and America during the second half of the 18th century. In industry, machines were invented for the manufacture of goods. Mills and factories were built, and people, who until then had mostly lived in the country, moved into the towns to work in industry. Slums grew up in the large manufacturing areas. Sewers became too small, few houses had lavatories, water was in short supply and garbage lay uncollected in the streets. Disease and death were all around.

However, two important advances were made. The first concerned an eight year old boy, James Phipps, a milkmaid, and a Gloucestershire doctor named Edward Jenner. Jenner had heard it said by country people that milkmaids who contracted cowpox never caught small-pox. On a historic occasion in 1796 he vaccinated James Phipps with pus from the milkmaid's cowpox sores then, several weeks later, with smallpox virus. The boy remained free of the dreaded disease. A similar system of vaccination was later successfully applied to other diseases.

The second advance was in the treatment of mental patients. Victims were kept in filthy conditions and treated with great cruelty. In 1796 a French doctor, Phillippe Pinel, was allowed to release fifty insane people from their chains and so took the first step to a better age in mental health.

Mental patients in an 18th century asylum

The relief of pain

Although a form of hypnotism had been practised in India, and the Romans sometimes used anaesthetic sponges, it is doubtful whether these ideas for easing pain had much real effect. As recently as one hundred and thirty years ago only external operations, such as amputations, were possible and these were occasions of utter horror for the patient. He, or she, would be strapped to a table or held down by assistants and the surgeon would cut and saw through the limb while the patient screamed in agony. Surgeons tried to work quickly so as not to prolong the torture.

In 1799, Sir Humphry Davy discovered that *nitrous oxide,* or 'laughing gas', helped to remove pain when breathed into the lungs and could make people temporarily unconscious. Forty years later Michael Faraday found that *ether* had the same effect. In 1844, two dentists showed that teeth could be painlessly extracted using 'laughing gas', and in 1846 a famous American surgeon of the time, John Warren, carried out a successful operation on a patient's throat using ether as an anaesthetic. In the following year *chloroform* was found to relieve pain during childbirth.

Many prominent people still frowned on the use of anaesthetics and it was not until Queen Victoria agreed to have chloroform at the birth of her seventh child that the controversy finally died away.

Dr. William Morton, who brought anaesthetics into general use, and his ether inhaler.

In 1847 chloroform was discovered at a supper party when James Simpson, of Edinburgh, and two friends experimented with various substances on themselves. All three were found unconscious on the floor.

Infection

A great advance in the relief of pain was made in the 19th century. This was the discovery of *cocaine* and its effectiveness as a local anaesthetic. It could be injected into a certain part of the body and deaden the pain in that part while an operation was performed, without the patient being put to sleep.

Now that the problem of pain had been solved, surgeons were able to carry out longer, more complicated operations. And there was no longer any need to hurry quite so much over the work. However, there were other problems. Soldiers still died from wounds which should have healed, and patients failed to survive apparently successful operations. Deaths in childbirth were numerous and occurred for no obvious reason.

At a hospital in Vienna it was noticed that doctors were assisting in the births of babies immediately after dissecting dead bodies in another room. It was thought that infection was being carried from the bodies to the babies on the doctor's hands and clothes. When the doctors were made to wash and change after dissection, the death-rate dropped.

However, no-one really knew what infection was, and that germs and viruses could enter the blood stream and prove fatal. Any such thoughts were met with disbelief and derision – most people thought that disease and contamination were spread by bad smells.

'Just one drop of city drinking water !' A 19th century cartoon reflecting the public's attitude of humour and disbelief regarding theories of unseen dangers of infection

Louis Pasteur

The greatest single contribution to medical history in the 19th century was made by a Frenchman named Louis Pasteur. He produced the theory that disease and infection were caused by germs and he proved that they were carried and spread, not by bad smells, but through the air.

Pasteur was a scientist, not a doctor, and he first discovered the action of germs whilst studying fermentation in wines and other liquids. He found that germs could be killed by applying heat to the liquids and the term *pasteur*isation was given to this process. Milk is treated in this way today to make sure it is safe to drink.

Germs are tiny living organisms which cannot be seen with the naked eye. By Pasteur's time the microscope had been invented and he was able to examine them. He discovered that different kinds of germs caused different diseases and he found a way of keeping them alive in his laboratory and even breeding them. Artificially made germs are known as *cultures*.

During an experiment on a disease in chickens he made another discovery. If he injected the chickens with a stale culture of the disease, they did not catch it but remained healthy even when fresh germs were injected. From this experiment our whole system of inoculation against disease has developed.

The lady with the lamp

In the 19th century there were basically two kinds of hospital: those run by voluntary contributions or under the patronage of some rich person, and those run by the State. Some of the voluntary hospitals, such as St. Bartholomew's and St. Thomas's in London, had been started much earlier in monasteries. Guy's Hospital was started under the patronage of a Thomas Guy. State hospitals were known as Poor Law Institutions or Workhouses where poor people went, very often to die.

Both kinds of hospital were mostly unhygienic, infectious and badly run. Nurses in those days worked from morning till night. Not only did they attend to the sick but also had to do all the domestic work in the wards. They had no uniforms, no training and rarely washed between such activities as floor-cleaning and nursing the patients.

During the Crimean War, Florence Nightingale and her team of devoted nurses did a great deal to improve the standard of nursing and patient welfare in the army hospitals. At night, carrying a lantern, she moved through the crowded wards to comfort and tend the wounded. She came to be known as 'the lady with the lamp'. On her return to Britain she set about improving conditions in civilian hospitals. She started the Nightingale School for Nurses and saw that the students were properly trained, strictly supervised and given uniforms.

Florence Nightingale supervising a new intake of wounded during the Crimean War

Safer surgery

Although some doctors still clung to bleeding as a remedy for numerous ills, many new drugs and techniques were being developed by the latter part of the 19th century. The surgeon was no longer a butcher or a barber but was now recognised as a skilled craftsman on an equal level with the doctor.

But surgery still had its problems and a patient's recovery was still mainly a matter of good luck. However, another great advance was made when a famous surgeon of that time, Joseph Lister, heard about the work of Louis Pasteur and his experiments showing that germs are present on and around everything. Lister decided that germs must be the cause of wound infections and of the failure of many operations. He set about cleaning and sterilising everything that had anything to do with an operation; the patient's skin, the surgeon's hands, instruments, sewing thread and swabs. Later on, instead of operating in their ordinary clothes, surgeons were required to wear special gowns and masks. Rubber gloves were invented in 1890. All these precautions made a tremendous difference and the hospital death-rate fell rapidly.

The way was now open for surgeons to perform more difficult internal operations, including even those on the brain. The development of blood transfusion added still further to the range of surgical possibilities. It has since saved hundreds of thousands of lives.

An operation in progress, using Lister's steam carbolic spray 1882

42

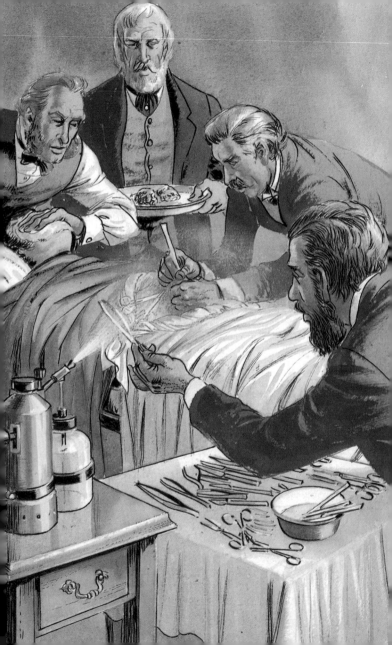

X-rays

At about the same time that surgeons were beating the germ menace in hospitals another important discovery was being made. It concerned a special, sealed glass tube from which the air had been withdrawn and through which an electric current was passed. *Cathode rays* were generated which caused the tube to glow. Experimenting with this equipment, a German professor named Röentgen found that it produced an invisible ray that would pass through quite thick substances. On placing his hand in front of the apparatus he saw that the rays passed through the flesh but cast a shadow of the bones on to a screen. Because he did not know what the rays were he called them X-rays. The significance of these rays in helping to diagnose internal complaints was quickly realised.

Today, X-rays are also used to cure deep-seated diseases such as cancer, but these are not produced in the same way as the rays which show up parts of the body. It is thanks to the devoted, and often dangerous, work of Madame Marie and Professor Pierre Curie in discovering radium and its 'radioactive' properties that our doctors and surgeons have this added weapon with which to combat malignant disease.

Wm. Röentgen 1895
Pierre and Marie Curie
Modern X-ray apparatus

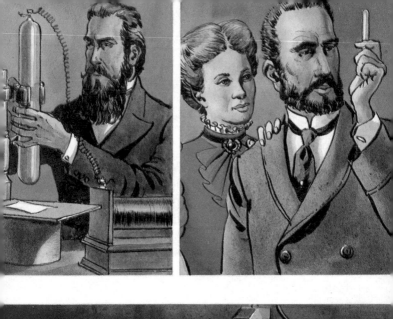
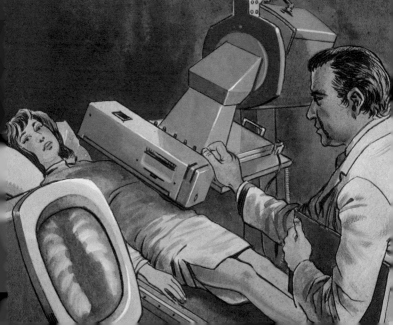

Into the 20th century

It can be said that in the 19th century more progress was made in the treatment of disease than in the preceding two thousand years. Indeed, the previous pages of this book show how many important discoveries were made.

However, at the beginning of the present century the family doctor was still working very much on his own, diagnosing ailments and treating them mainly from the contents of his 'little black bag'. As time went on he became a member of a team. He was able to draw on the knowledge of people who specialised in various diseases, chemists, research workers and laboratory technicians.

The problem of payment still remained. Medical services cost money and those who needed them most were often the very ones who could least afford them. At first various insurance systems were introduced to help meet the cost, and then in 1948 the National Health Service was launched, bringing medical and surgical treatment within the range of everyone in Britain. Some countries have a similar service while in others people still receive medical attention on a fee-paying and insurance basis.

While most of the old killer diseases have been brought under control, this century has produced its own occupational ailments. Cancer in its various forms has yet to be mastered.

A family doctor in the 1920's

More discoveries

During the first seventy years of the present century many discoveries were made both in the cure and prevention of disease.

Some diseases are not caused by germs or infections but by the lack of certain substances in our food. The discovery of vitamins in 1912 was a notable step in providing people with a properly balanced diet.

In 1921, insulin was extracted from a gland near the stomach of a dog and has helped to bring diabetes under control. A drug known as *sulphanilamide* was discovered in 1935. It became the first of the 'miracle' drugs which gained immediate and amazing results in the treatment of many infectious diseases, including pneumonia.

Penicillin was discovered in 1928 by Dr. Alexander Fleming, but no great use was made of it until the Second World War when it was used extensively to reduce infection in wounds. Today it is an essential part of a doctor's armament against infection. Penicillin was followed by streptomycin and a series of anti-infection drugs known as antibiotics.

During the two World Wars, great advances were made in the techniques of plastic surgery in which skin, bone or muscle taken from one part of the body is grafted on to a badly injured area in another part. In this way, terrible injuries can be 'mended' and new features built up.

Above -
Sir Alexander Fleming, the discoverer of penicillin and Nobel Prize winner.

Left -
Penicillin mould as seen under a microscope.

Machines and 'spare part' surgery

Our story of medicine began in prehistoric times and has taken us through ages of superstition and horror, through short periods of advance and enlightenment and centuries of ignorance and disbelief. We have now come to an era of fantastic progress in which machines are made to reproduce body functions and human organs are passed on from one person to another.

A wonderful recent invention was the *artificial kidney*. This carries out the function of a patient's own kidneys while they are being rested or operated upon, or if they cease to function.

The *heart-lung* machine takes over the work of a patient's heart and lungs during a heart operation and enables the surgeon to carry out his intricate work without hurry.

In recent years medical science has increased the knowledge of how to transplant certain organs from a person recently dead into a living person whose own organs are diseased. In special cases of blindness the transplanting of the *cornea* of the eye can bring back sight to the living. Kidneys can be replaced, and now heart transplanting is being undertaken.

Transplanting, or 'spare part' surgery, is still in its infancy. Who knows what the story of medicine will tell a hundred years from now!

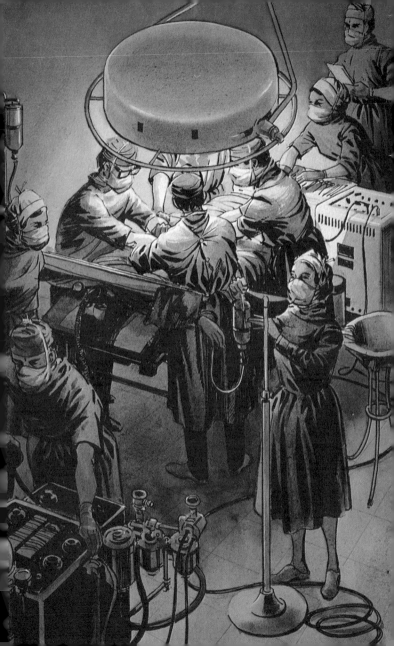

A Ladybird Achievements Book
Series 601